NEVER GIVE UP!

DATE:___/___/___

"You were given this life because you are strong enough to live it!" - Unknown

never give up

DATE:___/___/___

think positive

"The best way to gain self-confidence is to do what
you are afraid to do." – Unknown

DATE:___/___/___

MAKE IT HAPPEN

DATE:___/___/___

think
positive

"Believe in miracles but above all believe in yourself!"

DATE:____/____/____

DATE:___/___/___

think positive

"Never downgrade your dreams, reach for the stars and believe in your self power"

DATE:____/____/____

BELIEVE IN YOURSELF

DATE:___/___/___

think
positive

"Never be afraid to start something new,
if you fail it is just temporary, if you believe and
persist you will succeed"

DATE:___/___/___

TAKE ACTION!

DATE:___/___/___

think
positive

"Wherever you go, go with all your heart." - Confucius

DATE:___/___/___

DATE:___/___/___

think positive

"Your dreams and your goals are the seeds
of your own success"

DATE:___/___/___

MAKE IT HAPPEN

DATE:___/___/___

think positive

"*Start where you are and take chances*"

DATE:____/____/____

"If you never give up you become unbeatable, just keep going!"

BELIEVE YOU CAN

DATE:___/___/___

think
positive

"Life isn't about finding yourself.
Life is about creating yourself." - George Bernard Shaw

DATE:___/___/___

BELIEVE IN YOURSELF

DATE:___/___/___

think positive

"CHANGE YOUR LIFE TODAY. DON'T GAMBLE ON THE FUTURE, ACT NOW, WITHOUT DELAY." — SIMONE DE BEAUVOIR

DATE:___/___/___

TAKE ACTION!

DATE:___/___/___

think
positive

"AIM FOR THE STARS TO KEEP YOUR DREAMS ALIVE"

DATE:___/___/___

"There are no limits to what you can achieve if you believe in your dreams"

never give up

DATE:___/___/___

think positive

"When you feel you are defeated, just remember,
you have the power to move on,
it is all in your mind"

DATE:____/____/____

MAKE IT HAPPEN

DATE: ___/___/___

think
positive

"OPPORTUNITY COMES TO THOSE WHO NEVER GIVE UP"

DATE:____/____/____

BELIEVE
YOU CAN

DATE:___/___/___

think positive

"ALWAYS AIM FOR BIGGER GOALS, THEY HAVE
THE POWER TO KEEP YOU MOTIVATED"

DATE:____/____/____

BELIEVE IN YOURSELF

DATE:___/___/___

think positive

"SUCCESS IS NOT A PLACE OR A DESTINATION,
IT IS A WAY OF THINKING WHILE ALWAYS
HAVING A NEW GOAL IN MIND"

DATE:____/____/____

*"Fall seven times and stand up eight." –
Japanese Proverb*

TAKE ACTION!

DATE: ___/___/___

think positive

"CHANGE THE WORLD ONE DREAM AT A TIME,
BELIEVE IN YOUR DREAMS"

DATE:_____/_____/_____

"*Dreams make things happen; nothing is impossible as long as you believe.*"

never
give
up

DATE:___/___/___

think
positive

"Never loose confidence in your dreams,
there will be obstacles and defeats, but you will
always win if you persist"

DATE:___/___/___

MAKE IT HAPPEN

DATE:＿＿/＿＿/＿＿

think
positive

"Never wait for someone else to
validate your existence, you are the
creator of your own destiny"

DATE:___/___/___

"Always dream big and follow your heart"

BELIEVE YOU CAN

DATE:___/___/___

think positive

"Everything you dream is possible
as long as you believe in yourself"

DATE:___/___/___

BELIEVE IN YOURSELF

DATE:___/___/___

think positive

"A SUCCESSFUL PERSON IS SOMEONE THAT UNDERSTANDS
TEMPORARY DEFEAT AS A LEARNING PROCESS, NEVER GIVE UP!"

DATE:___/___/___

TAKE ACTION!

_____

_____

_____

_____

_____

_____

_____

_____

_____

_____

_____

_____

_____

_____

_____

_____

_____

_____

DATE:___/___/___

think
positive

"MOTIVATION COMES FROM WORKING ON OUR DREAMS AND
FROM TAKING ACTION TO ACHIEVE OUR GOALS"

DATE:___/___/___

DATE:____/____/____

think positive

"your mission in life should be to thrive
and not merely survive"

DATE:___/___/___

MAKE IT HAPPEN

DATE:___/___/___

think positive

"DOING WHAT YOU BELIEVE IN, AND GOING AFTER YOUR DREAMS WILL ONLY RESULT IN SUCCESS." - ANONYMOUS

DATE:____/____/____

BELIEVE YOU CAN

DATE:___/___/___

think positive

"The will to win, the desire to succeed, the urge to reach your full potential... these are the keys that will unlock the door to personal excellence." – Confucius

DATE:____/____/____

BELIEVE IN YOURSELF

DATE:___/___/___

think positive

"LET YOUR DREAMS BE BIGGER THAN YOUR FEARS AND YOUR ACTIONS
LOUDER THAN YOUR WORDS." - ANONYMOUS

DATE:___/___/___

TAKE ACTION!

DATE:____/____/____

think positive

"START EVERY DAY WITH A GOAL IN MIND AND
MAKE IT HAPPEN WITH YOUR ACTIONS"

DATE:____/____/____

DATE:___/___/___

think positive

"If you have big dreams you will always
have big reasons to wake up every day"

DATE:___/___/___

MAKE IT HAPPEN

DATE:___/___/___

think
positive

"Difficulties are nothing more than
opportunities in disguise, keep on
trying and you will succeed"

DATE:___/___/___

BELIEVE YOU CAN

DATE:___/___/___

think
positive

"Always have a powerful reason to wake up
every new morning, set goals and follow your dreams"

DATE:___/___/___

BELIEVE IN YOURSELF

DATE:___/___/___

think positive

"NEVER LET YOUR DREAMS DIE FOR FEAR OF FAILURE.
DEFEAT IS JUST TEMPORARY: YOUR DREAMS ARE YOUR POWER"

DATE:___/___/___

TAKE ACTION!

DATE:___/___/___

think positive

"A FAILURE IS A LESSON, NOT A LOSS. IT IS A TEMPORARY
AND SOMETIMES NECESSARY DETOUR, NOT A DEAD END"

DATE:___/___/___

DATE:___/___/___

think
positive

"Never let your doubt blind your goals, for your future lies in your ability, not your failure" — *Anonymous*

DATE:___/___/___

MAKE IT HAPPEN

DATE:___/___/___

think positive

"Laughter is the shock absorber that softens and
minimizes the bumps of life" — Anonymous

DATE:___/___/___

BELIEVE YOU CAN

DATE:___/___/___

think positive

"HOPE IS A WAKING DREAM" - ARISTOTLE

DATE:___/___/___

BELIEVE IN YOURSELF

DATE: ___/___/___

think positive

"NEVER GIVE UP ON A DREAM JUST BECAUSE OF THE TIME IT WILL TAKE
TO ACCOMPLISH IT. THE TIME WILL PASS ANYWAY."
– ANONYMOUS

DATE:___/___/___

TAKE ACTION!

DATE:___/___/___

think positive

"IF YOU WANT TO FEEL RICH, JUST COUNT ALL THE THINGS
YOU HAVE THAT MONEY CAN'T BUY" — ANONYMOUS

DATE:_____/_____/_____

"It does not matter how slowly you go as long as you do not stop" – Confucius

think
positive

"Some pursue success and
happiness – Others create it"
— Anonymous

DATE:____/____/____

MAKE IT HAPPEN

DATE:___/___/___

"IT'S BETTER TO HAVE AN IMPOSSIBLE DREAM THAN
NO DREAM AT ALL" — ANONYMOUS

DATE:___/___/___

BELIEVE YOU CAN

think positive

"The winner always has a plan; The loser always has an excuse" — Anonymous

DATE:___/___/___

BELIEVE IN YOURSELF

DATE:___/___/___

think positive

"There is no elevator to success.
you have to take the stairs"
— Anonymous

DATE:___/___/___

TAKE ACTION!

DATE:___/___/___

think positive

"DON'T LET YESTERDAY'S DISAPPOINTMENTS, OVERSHADOW
TOMORROW'S ACHIEVEMENTS" — ANONYMOUS

DATE:____/____/____

DATE:___/___/___

think positive

"WE ARE LIMITED, NOT BY OUR ABILITIES, BUT BY OUR VISION"
— ANONYMOUS

DATE:___/___/___

"The mind is everything. What you think you become." – Buddha

DATE:___/___/___

think positive

"A JOURNEY OF A THOUSAND MILES MUST BEGIN
WITH A SINGLE STEP." – LAO TZU

DATE:___/___/___

BELIEVE YOU CAN

DATE:____/____/____

think positive

"A diamond is a chunk of coal that
made good under pressure"
— Anonymous

DATE:___/___/___

BELIEVE IN YOURSELF

DATE:___/___/___

think positive

"REMEMBER YESTERDAY, DREAM OF TOMORROW, BUT
LIVE FOR TODAY" — ANONYMOUS

DATE:___/___/___

"Wherever you go, go with all your heart" – Confucius

TAKE ACTION!

DATE:___/___/___

think
positive

"Dream is not what you see in sleep, dream is the thing
which does not let you sleep" — Anonymous

DATE:_____/_____/_____

"All our tomorrows depend on today" — Anonymous

DATE:___/___/___

think positive

"DON'T BE PUSHED BY YOUR PROBLEMS.
BE LED BY YOUR DREAMS" — ANONYMOUS

DATE:____/____/____

MAKE IT HAPPEN

DATE:___/___/___

think positive

"ONCE YOU HAVE A DREAM PUT ALL YOUR HEART
AND SOUL TO ACHIEVE IT"

DATE:___/___/___

BELIEVE YOU CAN

DATE:___/___/___

think positive

"YOU CREATE YOUR LIFE BY FOLLOWING
YOUR DREAMS WITH DECISIVE ACTIONS"

DATE:___/___/___

BELIEVE IN YOURSELF

DATE:___/___/___

think positive

"The road to success is always full of surprises
and temporary failures, real success comes
to those who persist and enjoy the journey"

DATE:___/___/___

TAKE ACTION!

DATE: ___/___/___

think
positive

"TO live a creative life, we must lose
our fear of being wrong"
- Anonymous

DATE:___/___/___

DATE:___/___/___

think positive

"MAKE EACH DAY COUNT, YOU WILL NEVER
HAVE THIS DAY AGAIN"

DATE:___/___/___

MAKE IT HAPPEN

DATE:___/___/___

think positive

"SUCCESSFUL PEOPLE MAKE A HABIT OF DOING WHAT
UNSUCCESSFUL PEOPLE DON'T WANT TO DO"
— ANONYMOUS

DATE:___/___/___

BELIEVE YOU CAN

think
positive

Be Strong! It might be stormy
now, but it can't rain forever!"
- Anonymous

DATE: ___/___/___

BELIEVE IN YOURSELF

DATE:_____/_____/_____

BELIEVE IN YOURSELF

"Be Strong! It might be stormy now,
but it can't rain forever!" - Anonymous

DATE:___/___/___

BELIEVE IN YOURSELF

BELIEVE IN YOURSELF

"You were given this life because you are strong enough to live it!" - Unknown

"It doesn't matter what you look like on the outside. It's what's on the inside that counts"
- Unknown

BELIEVE IN YOURSELF

DATE:___/___/___

BELIEVE IN YOURSELF

DATE:___/___/___

BELIEVE IN YOURSELF

DATE:____/____/____

BELIEVE IN YOURSELF

DATE:____/____/____

"Be Strong – Be Brave – Keep Going"

BELIEVE IN YOURSELF

DATE:_____/_____/_____

BELIEVE IN YOURSELF

DATE:___/___/___

BELIEVE IN
YOURSELF

WE HOPE YOU LIKED YOUR JOURNAL - NOTEBOOK
PLEASE WRITE YOUR REVIEW, IT MEANS A LOT TO US!

DESIGNED BY:

CREATIVE JOURNALS FACTORY

THANK YOU!

Made in the USA
Coppell, TX
27 March 2021